Police Officers

by Shannon Knudsen

D1528590

Lerner Publications Company • Minneapolis

MASTICS-MORICHES-SHIRLEY
COMMUNITY LIBRARY

Text copyright © 2005 by Lerner Publishing Group, Inc.

All rights reserved. International copyright secured. No part of this book may be reproduced,
stored in a retrieval system, or transmitted in any form or by any means—electronic, mechanical,
photocopying, recording, or otherwise—without the prior written permission of Lerner Publishing
Group, Inc., except for the inclusion of brief quotations in an acknowledged review.

Lerner Publications Company
A division of Lerner Publishing Group, Inc.
241 First Avenue North
Minneapolis, MN 55401 U.S.A.

Website address: www.lernerbooks.com

Words in **bold type** are explained in a glossary on page 30.

Library of Congress Cataloging-in-Publication Data

Knudsen, Shannon, 1971–
    Police officers / by Shannon Knudsen.
      p.   cm. – (Pull ahead books)
    Includes index.
    ISBN-13: 978–0–8225–1693–4 (lib. bdg. : alk. paper)
    ISBN-10: 0–8225–1693–4 (lib. bdg. : alk. paper)
    ISBN-13: 978–0–8225–2534–9 (pbk. : alk. paper)
    ISBN-10: 0–8225–2534–8 (pbk. : alk. paper)
    1. Police–Juvenile literature. I. Title. II. Series.
HV7922.K58 2005
363.2–dc22   2004002623

Manufactured in the United States of America
3 4 5 6 7 8 – BP – 13 12 11 10 09 08

Look out! That car is going too fast!
Who can stop it?

Police officers can help. They work to keep their **community** safe.

A community's police officers belong to the same **police department.** What jobs do police officers do?

On busy streets, officers direct cars and trucks. Then drivers can stop, go, and turn safely.

Sometimes cars crash. Police officers rush to the scene to help. They call for help if anyone is hurt.

Police officers fight crime too.
Someone has robbed this store. The
store's owner calls the police.

An officer asks questions. What did
the robbers look like? Which way did
they run?

This police officer thinks he has found one of the robbers. The officer makes an **arrest.**

The arrested person is put in handcuffs and taken to the **police station.**

Police officers also try to find stolen things. A police officer might be able to get a stolen car back to the owner.

This police officer zooms along a highway on a motorcycle. A speedy motorcycle can catch unsafe drivers.

Many officers work in police cars.

A police car has flashing lights and loud **sirens.** They warn drivers to pull over and let the police car pass.

Bikes help some police officers do their jobs.

Bikes can go places where cars can't.

Some police officers work on foot.
They walk the streets. They offer help
and make sure people are safe.

This police officer rides a horse.
On horseback, police officers sit tall.
What other animal works with police?

Dogs do police work. Police dogs and their officers are called **K-9 units.** The dogs can sniff out drugs and bombs.

Being a police officer can be
dangerous. How do officers stay
safe? One way is to stay in touch.

Police officers use radios to talk to each other. Officers can call for help if they need it.

Many police officers work with a
partner. Partners help each other to
watch for trouble.

Police officers carry weapons.
Sometimes a gun or a stick called a
baton can save an officer's life.

How can you tell if someone is a police officer? Look for a **uniform.** Uniforms are special clothes that match.

All police officers have a **badge.** A
badge shows the officer's number and
the name of the police department.

Police officers work hard to help us stay safe.

They are important helpers in every community.

Facts about Police Officers

- Some police officers do not wear uniforms. These officers work in plain clothes. They try to surprise people who are committing crimes.

- Transit police help keep people safe when they are going places. Transit police ride on buses, subways, and trains to protect passengers.

- Police officers aren't always on the street. Some officers visit schools to teach people how to stay safe and look out for one another.

- Some police are scientists. They work in laboratories and study clues to help officers solve crimes.

- The most famous police officers in Canada are the Royal Canadian Mounted Police. They are also called Mounties. The Mounties are known for their bright red coats and their horses.

Police Officers through History

Hundreds of years ago, most communities did not have police officers or police departments. In some communities, soldiers did the jobs of police officers. The first soldiers who did the jobs of police officers lived in Rome, Italy, more than 2,000 years ago.

- How did people stay safe in areas without soldiers or police officers? Some places had a sheriff who helped catch people who broke the law. Most people just watched out for trouble for themselves and their neighbors. If someone committed a crime in a home or business, neighbors came to help.

- In 1750, a man named Henry Fielding banded together some officers to form the Bow Street Runners in London, England. Then Sir Robert Peel started a police department in London in 1829. The first city police department in the United States was formed in New York City in 1845. Over time, other cities started police departments too.

Glossary

arrest: a way that police can stop a person who is breaking a law or acting in a way that may hurt others

badge: a metal pin that shows a police officer's department and number

baton: a stick that some police carry to protect themselves

community: a group of people who live or work near each other

K-9 units: dogs and police officers who work together

police department: a group of police who work in the same community

police station: a building where police work together

sirens: the parts of police cars that make loud warning sounds

uniform: matching clothes that police officers wear

Index

About the Author

Shannon Knudsen writes and edits children's books. She lives in Minneapolis, Minnesota, with her two cats.

Photo Acknowledgments

The photographs in this book appear courtesy of: © Photodisc by Getty Images, front cover; © Mikael Karlsson, pp. 3, 4, 14, 20, 26; © James Leynse/Corbis, p. 5; © Todd Strand/Independent Picture Service, pp. 6, 8, 10, 11, 21, 27; © Andrew Stawicki/Zuma Press, p. 7; © Michael Heller/911 Pictures, p. 9; © Mikael Karlsson/911 Pictures, p. 12, 19; © Corbis Royalty Free, pp. 13, 15, 17, 22; © Earl & Nazima Kowall/Corbis, p. 18; © Jim West, p. 16, 23; © Tom Carter/911 Pictures, p. 24; © Annie Griffiths Belt/Corbis, p. 25.